The Accounting Book

By Michael Thomas

The Accounting Book

By Michael Thomas

Shoestring Book Publishing

The Accounting Book

Published by Shoestring Book Publishing

Paperback

ISBN: 9781500267889

Copyright 2014
By, Michael Thomas

This brochure was prepared for informational purposes only. The materials contained herein are not intended to, and do not constitute professional advice. Readers should not act upon this information without seeking professional counsel. Representation can only be accomplished by personally contacting this office and obtaining an agreement to represent. Reading this brochure does not constitute our agreement to provide representation.

This is a work of fiction. Names, characters, businesses, places, events and incidents are either the products of the author's imagination or used in a fictitious manner. Any resemblance to actual persons, living or dead, or actual events is purely coincidental.

Layout and design by Shoestring Book Publishing.

For information address:
Shoestringpublishing4u@gmail.com
www.shoestringbookpublishing.com

Acknowledgements:

For my special friends, Allan Emery and Alison Wakefield and their company Shoestring Book Publishing, I write this thank you for doing things that exceed the boundaries of caring. The formatting and suggestions for all elements of my books are often greater than the authorship. The depth of both of your knowledge is as if we are partners and I thank you so very much.

Michael

Table of Contents

Introduction:

This is quite a different book than I think I have ever seen. This is a book about the accounting of running a business, but, instead of just the usual charts and graphs that delineate how to run a business, it offers anecdotes on why to run a business and how to run it.

An old jeweler I once knew used to say; "You make the money and you never, ever let the money make you!" His contention was that if you chased money for money's sake it would consume you, change you. If you sought money for a reasonable purpose, then that money would be a good thing and you could justify your investment of time and self.

The problem with small business usually comes when they begin to become large businesses. It takes an entirely different demeanor to run a large business; the amount of dollars being thrown around, make it tempting to change your standards. But your standards are what put you where you are! They are the reason your small business was a success. You may have to change your methods of operation, but there is never a reason to change your moral or ethical standards!

This book attempts to give both the organic and inorganic wisdom needed to keep a small business afloat and make it flourish. Kick back and internalize everything in this book and you will understand how to make a small business thrive in this bohemian state.

Allan Emery

Executive Editor

Chapter One:
Starting a Business

Nothing in life can be as gruesome as all the work it takes to serve other people. Most business ventures start very shaky and all of them reflect the owners care. The cornerstone of any business is the heart to be honest which returns honesty back to you.

When you are starting a business one of the most important things to do, beforehand, is to walk the streets, talk to others, read books, go on line and gather as much information about your future business, as you can. When I started my business, I bound together a group of CPAs into monthly meeting sessions where we discussed common problems.

Those members are still my friends after years gone by. I can still call any one of them with questions. This network of competitors was more important than new client networks. I built my firm by being generous to Non Profits, Churches and such. Those endeavors returned to me a hundredfold.

There are so many pointers and cautions, but all business ventures will progress at the pace of the owner's objectivity and level of growth. This brochure was prepared for informational purposes only. The materials contained herein are not intended to, and do not constitute professional advice. Readers should not act upon this information without seeking professional counsel. Representation can only be accomplished by personally contacting this office and obtaining an agreement to represent. Reading this brochure does not constitute our agreement to provide representation.

1974 was a time to start a business for the four monks Pretend, as they may; they became what they were before they professed wisdom.

Mitchell created software and played music for fun. Kevin was a carpenter with Sonny and the fourth monk was named, Michael, me, an accountant.

Astrology software created by Mitchell was based upon the Babylonian twelve houses which were underpinned by the ephemeris or positioning of planetary objects reduced to mathematical configurations. Each of the sun signs fit into a house and each house had a specific meaning. Mitchell was the very best in the world at applying the ephemeris to extract meaning on reading charts. His small business started as a sole proprietor and quickly grew into a C-Corporation with an uncomplicated bookkeeping system overseen by Margo his wife. I did his taxes and was his pseudo friend. A friend, who simply saw him once a month to convert his bookkeeping into financial statements, I also learned to create astrological charts with Mitchell's help. Seeing Mitchell once a month was an endurance test. His taxes were easy and Mitchell had plans for me that I never bought into. He wanted me to create accounting software for him that he could sell to Microsoft. I was not interested and that became a sore point between us. The creation of software is a two-step process – one of creation and two of updating the software for the rest of that software's life. I did not want to be tied to one software package for that long of a period. Besides this was the fact that Mitchell was a professed Buddhist as I was also. And his main function, by my thoughts, was astrological software and he was veering from the path of what God gave him in abilities.

Now, how does "starting a business" relate to Mitchell on a continuing basis? Well Mitchell was not happy refining his astrology software since it generated enough revenue for him to relax. He never updated that astrology software to make it better and more "user friendly". That software still, to this day, is not easy to use and it could be made so, if Mitchell cared.

Mitchell realized that I was not going to create accounting software so he paid for a husband and wife team to come from Russia and live permanently in a house he bought for them. That couple, under Mitchell's supervision, created the now famous "Complete Music Guide" or "CMG" that is one of the most used book of music reviews of all genres of music.

Mitchell took an inadequate idea from a small company and made it the "Complete Music Guide" then completely lost the patent to it by being sued by the small company that started the inadequate version of the book. The main topic sentence dealing with Mitchell losing the patent is that he did not follow any Buddhist wisdom by getting an agreement with the small company who started the idea. Only Mitchell had the skills to implement the book in its final form. If he had shared the revenue with the small company, they never would have sued him and taken the patent away from him. In the end he lost, even though his name appears on the historical information. I believe he does not receive the revenue or all of the revenue from the sale of the book I lost track of Mitchell when, after almost eighteen years of helping him, I severed my relationship with him.

His "Transmission" that he was so proud of receiving in New York from the head of one of the main societies either the Amitabha or Mahayana Buddhist society, I do not know which one, during a world conference where he was singled out by the head of the society by passing the honor to Mitchell with a small slap in the face.

Mitchell took this honor, as being the next in line, to his head and became an unbearable ego centered burden to all he came into contact with. He never realized how he hurt people's feelings. He just acted as if he was above common courtesies. I found him so distasteful that I decided to disassociate myself from him. My therapist chides me in cautioning that all people have a "god centered core" and I was told to learn to recognize that part of people and not their exterior behavior, if I was to continue to practice spiritualism. I know I must learn to accept Mitchell as he is and it is hard for me since I consider him not acting in a "centered" or "balanced" manner. Mitchell, I apologize for being critical of you and, if you remember, years ago when you told me to "start a business" of my own as a CPA because I was good at being critical of people I took your advice and now have a corporation, like you, but I miss talking to you and being your friend.

Chapter Two:
Creating A Business Plan

The basic elements of a business plan start with a simple three ring binder with tab indexes that follow this sequence somewhat:

1.) Autobiography of owners/inceptors

2.) Short summation of the venture and it's goals

3.) Administrative tab with possible sub tabs:

    a.) Management Agreement

    b.) Current financial statements

    c.) Budgeted financial statements

    d.) Projected financial statements

    e.) Product tab describing what it is the company offers to it's customers

    f.) Marketing tab describing how the company will spread the word

4.) Miscellaneous tab with sub tabs:

    a.) Initial tax filings,

    b.) applications and/or copies of stock certificates

***

Kevin lived in a Buddhist home in Ann Arbor and kept the home repaired using his construction skills. He, Mitchell, Sonny and myself started out as aspiring monks.

Kevin worked, mainly with Sonny as a team or as partners and they started "Plainfolk Carpentry" together.

The name can still be found on line as an "inactive" company. I helped set up their business plan, initially Kevin met and married Leslie and they lived together creating three children and continued operating "Plainfolk Carpentry" together Sonny drifted off to start a Buddhist monastery in Detroit.

The business plan for Kevin and Leslie was simple and included them working in unison to do the three things a business plan involves: 1) Administrative or all the details related to running a business that are incidental to the main function of construction. 2) Product or what the company offers the general public, which was remodeling and building homes for "Plainfolk Carpentry". 3) Advertising or promoting the company as in what area and what customer group to focus on selling services to.

I watched their little company grow with employees and a reputation that favored them by being accepted as the "President" of the "Builders and Remodelers Association of Greater Ann Arbor". I attended the ceremony installing them both into their esteemed positions.

It was their notoriety that landed them big remodeling jobs. One large job resulted in a deposit of over $200,000 and they took the deposit to Las Vegas and lost the whole thing. There was never a mention in their business plan to gamble the company money.

Because of their actions, they were removed from their positions with the Ann Arbor builders society. They were sued and lost their company and, eventually, Kevin came around to selling phone services.

It is hard for me to not preach to them that they should have followed Buddhist or spiritual guidelines, but they strayed into worldly ways and here is what I believe: It is impossible to not be part of the world and its ways. But it is possible to be spiritual at the same time and stay apart from the worldly ways or not let the worldly ways take over your soul.

Chapter Three: Choice of Entity

Any company can have losses. As long as the owner is not a hobby company, losses are fully deductible every year with very little limitation. This company is called a "For Profit" venture. A hobby has requirements as to time devoted, size, procedures of administration and conducting the business before it can be upgraded to a "For Profit" venture.

Remember: In the early stages of your business it is always best to "start slow". It is easy to incorporate but it is much harder to get rid of a corporation once filed with the government. There are three choices of "For Profit" structures:

1) Sole Proprietor with possible LLC (entity ignored designation with IRS).

2) Partnership with possible LLC designation or added name and protection.

3) Corporation with possible LLC designation added name giving no added protection.

Two types of corporations:

S-Corporation or

C-CorporationNow,

Of these three types of "Entities" there are two categories of these above "Entities":

Pass-thru entities

or Non-pass thru entities.

All of the above are pass through entities except the C-Corporation. Pass through means that the profits or losses of the entity are passed through onto the personal tax returns of the owners. The way you get money out of a C-Corporation is by salary, commissions, rents, interest, etc. There are many, many reasons for choosing one type of entity over another. Each group of persons has different reasons for consideration of entity choice.

Three of the differences between pass-thru entities and a C-Corporation can be described as tax benefits of a C-Corporation:

> 1) C-Corporations allow the owners to deduct all medical insurance.

> 2) C-Corporations allow the owners to deduct all medical bills not paid by insurance.

> 3) C-Corporations have a very low tax rate—25% for earnings up to $75,000.

Most of the large corporations of America are C-Corp. For a corporation to be C-Corporation much planning has to be in place to insure a long term strategy to deal with the sale of C-Corp.

Sonny was a handsome person. In his Buddhist robe and sandals he typified a holy person in looks. He met Pamela, a Buddhist pilgrim and they married. Under their guidance they started a non-profit organization that became the "Meditative Buddhist Temple" in Ann Arbor. It was with much discussion that they chose to not be a corporation or partnership. They were wise and easy to guide by their open-minded attitude.

Sonny worked with Kevin and "Plainfolk Carpentry", to keep the Temple in repair and expand into two attached houses on Packard Avenue with a lovely brick entrance. Aspirants lived in the community of houses and grew with the physical expansion Sonny and Patricia had children and a sense of peace overlay their association together.

Part of their choice of entities afforded them to not pay taxes as a not-for-profit business, and they grew.

One of the resident students was Sandra, a young woman who fell in love with Sonny and with her, he left Ann Arbor and went to California for a number of years. Pamela became the head of the Temple and raised her children without her husband. She rose in stature to be the most capable of persons who controlled the whole Buddhist community in Ann Arbor and kept it in place with her administrative skills. I was so proud of her abilities and watched as time ensued and her husband returned begging a place in her successful life. She refused him. He still put himself out as a Buddhist monk and brought his girlfriend back from California and lived openly with her. Pamela divorced him. He moved to Detroit and set up the "Detroit Buddhist Center" with his girlfriend in a small house in the "New Center" area of the city. He came to me to do his taxes and I had to refuse him out of loyalty to Pamela and her Temple. I felt so sorry for him because he was a sad person who had followed an incorrect path and was trying to recover.

As part of my education in choosing an entity, I learned one important thing: When I told this story to my publisher, he said, it is mandatory that one choose the "path with heart" in order to be successful.

Chapter Four:
Bookkeeping

1) Sole Proprietorships or start-up small business ventures can often get by this way:

   (a) if the name of the company is the same name of the person

(b) if there are usually less than twenty or thirty checks being written per month.

Then the personal checking account of the taxpayer can have intermingled personal and business checks in it. IRS does not dictate bookkeeping. Secret of this simple method is to copy the check register. Highlight the business deposits and checks. Summarize only those highlighted for tax purposes.

2) Deeper more complicated bookkeeping will usually demand federal identification numbers, separate bank accounts and complicated software. Before we get into software, let us assume we do not qualify for above; well the next hand type of bookkeeping is what I did for years—spread sheet bookkeeping. As simple as an Excel spreadsheet with columns for categories such as "office/telephone/etc". And lines for the information of check-by-check. This is real easy bookkeeping and at the end of the year you simply add the columns.

3) Quicken comes free with a lot of computers. It is the next choice for a simple computer program that summarized the transactions easily.

4) Software steps up to Quick Books which is the most predominant across the country. Costs about $200 and it works well without user being an accountant.

5) Remember, Frater Luca Bartolomeo Pacioli in 1486 invented the double entry bookkeeping method. Ever since, everyone runs around afraid of debit and credit. Yet, the simple formula is that if you put in once in the left side (of a two column) you have to put it in the right side, so that both sides balance. Teeter Totter, yea.

***

Cousin Eddie figured I would fall right in line, after Viet Nam laundering his mob money. He heard that I was working in a CPA firm and told me that he wanted his Dry Cleaner's books to be done by me. Word went back to him, through cousin Esse, that I refused. Esse warned me that he did not take being refused, too lightly. I told Esse to apologize to him and the threat went away.

Bookkeeping is so simple, to us who know it as a profession. To others, it is a mystery.

We know that all Government FBI or CIA agents must be lawyers and Certified Public Accountants because most crime prosecuted is discovered through the books of illegal organizations. The old maxim: "Follow the money" is mostly true. It would be too complicated to say: "Follow the debits and credits".

Luca Pacioli in the 1400's created double entry bookkeeping. Luca never did any books for Mique who had a hair salon. I did her books once a month for $35.00. The simple hand posted books back in 1970 were columnar two-post sheets that spread out on each side to about 24 columns. This system was the precursor to VisiCalc which came before Microsoft Excel. It was always a joy creating books by hand and I enjoy Quick Books but I wish for the old days. Of course Mique did not care about these things as long as I kept her books correctly and filed her taxes on time. At Mique's salon I worked upstairs in a little room with windows.

I was told by my friends that the house where Mique rented and conducted her salon, which had several rooms, was used as a house of prostitution in the past. Mique used to come up to the room where I did my bookkeeping. She would ask me why I did not want to take advantage of the ladies she hired as prostitutes. I never asked Mique if she put the money from the ladies into the salon bank account. I will tell you this, Mique was the princess of wild parties and every weekend there was a party of liquor and drugs that Mique held. She was the center of the party scene in Ann Arbor. She was always trying to get me to one of her parties. I just knew if I ever attended one of her parties, I would never ever remember which side of the books were debits or credits. I would forget bookkeeping and want to party every week.

Chapter Five:
Initial Investment

When you start a business you are allowed to deduct any expenses related to the new business. If you go back in time and find assets and costs that you paid for but you do not have receipts for these expenditures, then estimate the cost and take photographs of the assets so as to verify the deduction only if you get asked by the government. Now, this list of expenses and their values must be reasonable according to market values and such other guidelines. And if you have partners, you should try to get accurate lists from all your partners. You should try to keep these partner lists somewhat equal, if possible. Once you have your list of monies spent for assets, software, classes, furniture, equipment and such, then you are allowed to do a journal entry and place these assets upon the books of the company, and have the company owe you the money back for the cost of these assets. This initial investment is sometimes forgotten.

***

This is a short chapter. When setting up a company, the new owner or owner needs to inventory books, computers and any item used to run the business and get credit for those items in exchange for either stock or note payable to the owner. Gerry Banks gave me his inventory and the early years of laser tools for contractors, engineers, rifle aiming devices and other uses of laser technology, Gerry Banks was a laser scientist and if I met with him to help set up his company, he would shut the shades and ask me to speak low because he believed that the U S Government was gathering evidence on him to arrest him for shipping laser devices to European customers. He shrouded his initial investment in "couched" language calling his laser inventory simply "equipment". Gerry never got arrested but I am sure he kept his investment items hidden from view.

I remember Sandy telling me that she wanted to call her investment items: "Big Stuff" and "Little Stuff" She named the automobile that she contributed to the business, "Toulouse" and I complied by entering it on the books as a "Toulouse Sedan". She used her little French made car for delivering.

I had a special case of a manufacturer of specialized grinding machinery who created a million dollar machine that did the grinding needed for a special auto part. The machine was used as a prototype and customers ordered from the specifics of the one machine. It was a special case because the investment was not a machine held for sale, only for showing customers how it worked. The personal property auditor, Catherine Scull finally agreed with me that the machine was not personal property but would eventually be sold. She was so understanding when I explained to her that the machine could not be taxed as a seven or eight year machine because eighty percent of the cost of the machine was "cutters" that did the grinding and the "cutters" wore out in one year. Can you imagine three quarter of a million dollars in simply knifes that cut the steel?

I will end this chapter by telling you of Bill and Bonnie who started their business on the heels of a man who disappeared from his business and eventually sold all the remaining special hard woods to Bill and Bonnie. The large inventory was always interesting to me since Bill would separate it by kind of trees, maple, elm, olive, pine, corktree, honey locust. The lovely odor of wood would entice me when we set up the initial investment for Bill and Bonnie to record when they set up their business. It is an earthy rich aroma. I used to enjoy Bill telling me where he acquired each lot of wood he had in inventory, either by visiting places where it was sold or finding it on line with his computer. The whole shop with its wood working equipment held that thick smell so deep with nature's smells.

Chapter Six:

Salary vs Contract Labor

	CORRECTED (if checked)	
PAYER's name, street address, city or town, province or state, country, ZIP or foreign postal code and telephone number	1 Rents 0.00	OMB No. 1545-0115
ABC Company, Inc. 61 Elmora Ave. STE 1 Elizabeth NJ 07202-1650 908-354-3441	2 Royalties 0.00 3 Other income 0.00	**2013** Form 1099-MISC
		4 Federal income tax withheld 0.00
PAYER'S Federal identification number 12-3456789	RECIPIENT'S identification number 125-67-5633	5 Fishing boat proceeds 0.00	6 Medical and health care payments 0.00
RECIPIENT's name Alfred E Newman Newman Contracting	7 Nonemployee compensation 65,000.00	8 Substitute payments in lieu of dividends or interest 0.00
Street address (including apt. no.) 125 River Rd	9 Payer made direct sales of $5,000 or more of consumer products to a buyer (recipient) for resale ▶ ☐	10 Crop insurance proceeds 0.00
City or town, province or state, country, and ZIP or foreign postal code Scotch Plains NJ 07066	11 Foreign tax paid 0.00	12 Foreign country/U.S. poss.
Account number (see IRS instructions)	13 Excess golden parachute payments 0.00	14 Gross proceeds paid to an attorney 0.00
15a Section 409A deferrals 0.00	15b Section 409A income 0.00	16 State tax withheld 0.00 / 0.00	17 State/Payer's state no. NJ 222468317000 / NY 123456789000	18 State income 0.00 / 0.00

a Control number 03-000240-	22222	void ☐ OMB No. 1545-0008		
b Employer identification number 99-6876543		1 Wages, tips, other compensation 25312.50	2 Federal income tax withheld 2622.33	
c Employer's name, address, and ZIP code Johnson Technical Services Corp 850 Tech Drive Suite 400 Anytown USA 15237		3 Social security wages 25312.50	4 Social security tax withheld 1569.38	
		5 Medicare wages and tips 25312.50	6 Medicare tax withheld 367.06	
		7 Social security tips	8 Allocated tips	
e Employee's social security number 221-00-9723		9 Advance EIC payment	10 Dependent care benefits	
d Employee's name, address, and ZIP code Dena T Brenner 179 Klein Road Arnold Pa 15068		11 Nonqualified plans	12a See instructions for box 12 D 120.00	
		13 ☐ ☐ ☐	12b	
		14 Other PA SUI 5.12	12c	
			12d	
15 State Employer's state ID number PA 5104C37D4	16 State wages, tips, etc. 25312.50	17 State income tax 708.79	18 Local wages, tips, etc. 25312.50	19 Local income tax 253.12	20 Locality name Allensburg

Form **W-2** Wage and Tax Statement   **2003**

Copy 1 For State, City, or Local Tax Department
Copy D For Employer.

Department of the Treasury - Internal Revenue Service
For Privacy Act and Paperwork Reduction Act Notice, see separate instructions.

Payroll taxes unpaid are the largest reason for business ventures to fail. Payroll tax problems are the one most time consuming element of my assistance to my clients. If you do not understand these last two sentences or if you do not understand the rules of paying employees, then you may as well never go in business for yourself.

The rule is simple - never get behind. If you hire contract laborers then you must have a folder for each and every one of them, and in that folder should be:

1.) Subcontract agreement (See me for examples. Have one drawn up by your attorney)
2.) Copy of drivers license.
3.) I-9 Department of Labor Form.
4.) Copy of social security card.
5.) Copy of persons' business card or any of their advertising brochures.
6.) Copy of w-9 form.

If you have all of the above, your chances of a sub-contractor, years later, telling the IRS that they were employees—this possibility becomes lessened. If a sub does complain to the IRS and you do not have all of the above things, then "Give Over" because the IRS will take their word.

If you hire employees your company should have an employee manual (see me for examples) If you hire employees you should have a folder as shown above for each and every employee as well as this:

1.) Becomes an employee agreement as spelled out in the company manual.

2.) Copy of W-4 exemption form signed by the employee

3.) Time card information and example If you have all of the above then your exposure for an employee suing you, becomes much less

***

Examples of conflict abound when an employee is put on payroll and has withholding taken out of their paycheck or they are given money with nothing taken out and the employee owes the tax normally paid by the employer.

Charlotte and Wayne had nice contracts to remodel for big companies. I did their bookkeeping and the employees used to bewail their designation as 1099 contract labor. The employees were college students holding their first job and they had their first lessons in reality when they owed taxes of upwards of fifteen thousand for withholding, both employer and employee portions of Medicare and Social Security. I tried talking to Charlotte into being understanding of the situation and she simply refused to discuss it. She was making money and shifted the tax to these unaware young people.

Now, it is true that the IRS will take the position of the employee who makes a complaint and usually force the employer to pay the taxes to the IRS that they should have established as regular employees for these people. The only trouble is that the young people, caught in these types of situations, are blackballed and cannot work in the area for years later after they turn their employer in for not being paid as an employee.

Charlie and Mary were the worst employers paying their employees as contract labor and issuing them 1099s. Charlie would hire uneducated young people or older men who needed a job severely to feed their families. Most all the time these unsuspecting people worked hard but had no idea that Charlie was going to do this to them till the year ended and they got a 1099 instead of a W2. In one particular year, Charlie built huge complexes of apartments with no payroll and over fifteen million dollars in contract labor paid to these unwary people who became desperate when the IRS charged them huge assessments for the taxes that Charlie and Martha did not pay.

I was fired as Charlie's CPA when I confronted Charlie and his wife telling them that they had a responsibility to these poor people and if they did not do the right thing, their company would not prosper and it did not do well over the long run. Coupled with all the other illegal things that Charlie and Mary were doing, the contract labor backfired on them and they could not get good help and the IRS caught up with them.

In my experience as a CPA, the 1099 versus W2 issue has been the most prominent problem in all of my business clients. The rule that you can get away with something some of the time, but never always, holds true. Usually if an employer hires over five or more people, they mostly always should do payroll.

Chapter Seven:
Cars and Trucks

1) Odometer reading needed at first of year and end of year. Odometer reading must be proven by print-out of repair facility record of your car for whole year. Or, copy of oil change or minor repair service.

2) Two readings are necessary: First of year. End of year.

3) No daily odometer readings are necessary during year.

4) A twelve month calendar must be kept of business miles by day, by name of client, as such, and total daily miles. Add up all the circled mileage by day, for the whole year.

 This, then:

a.) Business Miles (From Calendar)

b.) Total Miles (From Odometer)

c.) Commute Miles (Added Up/Estimated)

d.) Other Miles (Inferred/Deduced)

5) Total business miles are then multiplied by 56 cents per mile to arrive at the expense allowed for auto and truck.

6) Alternate method of auto and truck expense: The actual cost of : Depreciation, Gas, Oil, Repairs, Washes, Insurance, Leases, etc. All of these costs are added up and higher of mileage or actual can be used.

7) Depreciation = normal wear and tear measured in $ allowed per year. The maximum allowed for passenger cars for first year is $2,960. Trucks and vans can be depreciated up to $25,000 in the first year.

Eisenhower's Interstate is our gift from this World War II general who became the 34th president of America. Over 48 thousand miles of connected roads spanning our country carrying over one quarter of all vehicles travelling at once.

The IRS told Jeremy that he did not drive 40,000 miles in one year. To prove it and get him out of the clutches of the government, I discovered an emission control document where Jeremy's mileage was recorded in the middle of the year. That document along with one oil change near the first part of the year, formed the evidence that he did drive that much for the insurance company he worked at. A salient fact was that his wife divorced him because he was never home.

William and his son James Reichenbach were audited one year and James told me, "You sit back and I will do the talking." The fact that William, James, William's girlfriend and James's girlfriend all had brand new Cadillac's on the books being depreciated was finally approved by the IRS because James told the auditor that there was no way his girlfriend and his dad's or either Bill or James could go to the job sites in Fords. The IRS explained that the government supplied their employees with Fords. Jim told the guy that was his problem, he should ask for a Cadillac. As the CPA for Bill and Jim, I sat back and laughed quietly. James knew that the real reason that the auditor allowed the four Cadillacs as legitimate is because I had the four people reimburse the corporation for a nominal amount for personal use. The IRS was surprised that I had taken such precaution but it saved the day and four people drove around in great big Cadillac's passing up little Fords with angry IRS agents.

Chapter Eight:
Depreciation

Depreciation is one of the most complicated or convoluted of all government laws. In all the years of our lives, we can almost count as many changes to this aspect of deduction. What I am going to suggest to all of my readers is to let it go till the end of the year or divide their asset purchases by seven years for internal purposes temporarily until your accountant gets around to doing your work, let the accountant decide upon this:

1) leaving the seven years alone, because during any year it can be reduced.

2) writing off the whole asset using the rule of Section 179, presently $108,000 for property, $25,000 for SUVs, $2,960 for cars.

3) using the MACRS rules—let your accountant do it, but usually equals a larger amount in the first years of the asset life and smaller as years pass.

Remember: You have the last say as to what the years life an asset can be depreciated. For example: If you buy big things and smash them against a wall to test their crash capabilities, then the life of those assets are only a few hours. IRS cannot deny you if you can prove your point.

***

Over a period of years the Congress and IRS has created volumes of paperwork and rules for depreciating assets that boils down to nonsense.

I follow my simple rule of straight line for either three to seven years of life for normal assets.

When Carter Builders changed accountants from me helping him, his new CPA's called me up and said the IRS was questioning him on depreciation. I told Mr. Carter that I would help him, even though he had another CPA. He said he would pay me. I took seven years of asset schedules and set up regular depreciation as MACRS, ACRS, 200% Declining Balance, 150% Declining Balance, Sum Of The Digits Depreciation, GAA Accounts, GDS Recovery Assets, ADS Rules, Section 179 Expensing, and Recapture Rules. I created a schedule for the seven years that included Alternate Minimum Tax and Regular Tax as well as Tax and Book Depreciation. When I got through there was no problem in coming up with the correct answer to his problem and the end result was that the IRS agreed with me and sent him his proper small refund. The client, Mr. Carter told me, confidentially, that he appreciated what I did and paid me well.

My buddy, James Yokum was ten years younger than me and he died at his desk. He trained with me after Viet Nam and he got agent orange and bad feet from the jungle. I slept every night like a new born for the year I was in Viet Nam. I used to tell Jim that either his large client, who kept him running all the time or the depreciation rules were going to kill him.

He used to tell me, "Michael, I do not know how you get away with using straight line for everything". I used to tell him, in so many words, how can you allow stupid rules guide you. Be practical, my friend and the IRS can never, fault you for depreciating assets using simple rules such as straight line over three or seven years life. Bottom line is that my friend died and in the end his hospital machine showed a "straight line" which was not just an indication of his death, but an indication that he should have used "straight line" depreciation, too.

Chapter Nine:
Buy/Sell
And Management Arrangements

A simple form of buy/sell agreement is writing with a friendly competitor to take your business over in case of your death; and for them to pay the survivors an agreed upon set amount. Stepping up, below is an outline for a buy/sell strategy plan as follows:

1) Pay for a professional valuation of the company.

2) Buy life insurance or cross life insurance.

3) Make the beneficiaries the ones who will survive the insured.

4) Immediately sign the shares of the company over and hold them in trust.

5) Actually or simultaneously draft up the buy/sell agreement with the following:

    a) provision for death

    b) provision for disagreement

    c) provision for departure or retirement

    d) provision for disability

    e) provision for dissolution

All these topics are lead-ins for discussion and elaborations that can be worked out in the writing of the agreement. All of these topics will have loose ends that must be addressed in the final working out of the written agreement.

A good friend who is a CPA says this to me, "Michael, no matter how well you plan, there are always things which arise that were not anticipated. The best we can hope for is to plan as efficiently as possible to attempt to avoid as many surprises as possible." I will add: Life is not meant to be perfect. The greatest gift of life is the ability to recover with grace and love from situations of seeming despair. That is the true mark of a humane wise business person.

***

Darry and Markar two specialists who did the lighting for the movie "Standing In The Shadows of Motown". They suddenly found a need for the buy/sell arrangement that they drew up in rough draft with me thirty years ago. Their attorney formalized it. Now, as they approach finding a buyer for their business, they discovered the agreement and were surprised that there were five salient points – death/disagreement/departure/disability and dissoultion.

Being wise people, years ago they split off part of their lighting equipment and sold it reasonably to Bob and Paul. They also bought a $300,000 generator to sustain the lighting during conditions when electricity was not available. Darry jokes that he and Mark are not dead yet: Will never argue: Have Bob and Paul built in as the next owners: And never seem to find time to relax, because they are so busy. In the process of updating their living trusts, they were so pleased that they did not have to spend thousands of dollars on a new buy/sell. If a buy/sell is done right then it will hold itself as assurance for many years. The secret of the buy/sell that Darry and Mark agree upon is that the life insurance to underwrite the death of each partner is solid and in place as their business runs smooth and the beneficiaries are the surviving spouses, in either case, and not the corporation, since they want the surviving widow to get the insurance as quick as possible.

Chapter Ten:
Valuations

Formal valuation by experts hired for the job

Semi-formal valuation by interested attorney or accountant

Informal valuation agreed upon by parties and arrived at by simple formulas.

An informal valuation between two factions can be as easy as: "We both agree that the business is worth $100,000 and we will both sign documents to that effect. Or, factions can use simple formulas such as:

(a) percent of sales

(b) percent of receivables and so on to arrive at a valuation.

Then both parties sign in agreement. The other forms of valuation depend upon who one hires to arrive at a third party, objective price for the business. Remember, the key to a valuation is that both parties agree regardless of what method was used. Most valuations are accompanied by life insurance where the next of kin or designated beneficiary receives the insurance money in place of the company paying the next of kin.

***

"What are we worth?" Stephen has been the corporate officer of five public companies. I was so honored to have been his CPA for over thirty years and watched him grow. The fact that he developed and obtained a patent for a medical industry product was impressive, but mainly his easy manner and kindness kept him affectionately tied to me.

His partners accepted my valuation of their business for purposes of selling their interests while the product held its highest value. Large public companies draw out many types of owners, mostly very smart people who know when to join or sell effectively.

In the early stages of my profession, I was offered a stock ownership in a company, in exchange for my work. I refused because the company was going public and the man who offered me stock was the executive officer and, novice, though I was, I understood insider trading and stayed away from any inducement. Eventually that executive officer went to jail and he called me asking why I had turned him in. He asked if I would write a letter in his favor for parole I told him, "Gilbert, I did not turn you in and, no, I will not write a letter because I have nothing to say in your favor. You are in jail because you forged a document that the IRS discovered due to its importance. To forge the name of a professor of Columbia University is pretty serious stuff, Gilbert." I truly felt sorry for this man who accepted wrong while knowing what was right.

To answer the question, "What are we worth", I will moralize that companies are worth the highest level of ethics that their officers and stockholders adhere to.

Index of IRS Form Numbers

Publication 334 Tax Guide For Small Business

Publication 463   Travel, Entertainment, Gift & Car Expenses

Publication 946 How To Depreciate Property

Form 8834   Tax Credits Cars

Form 8910   Tax Credits Cars

Form 8863   Tax Credits Lifetime Learning Credit

Form 3800   General Business Credit

Form 6765   Credit For Increasing Research Activities

You can find these forms at: www.irs.gov

Also By Michael Thomas

The Plantagenets

Rabbi Schlotz Stories

Michael Thomas Poetry

Michael Thomas Poetry 2

Available at Amazon.com!

Author's Biography

Michael G. Thomas is a CPA residing and working in Canton and Ann Arbor, Michigan who is best described as a warm and cuddly curmudgeon. He has been writing for decades, primarily poetry and short stories, but has a love of plays and theatre. Mostly, he defies description, not because he is nondescript, but because the proper words have not been invented. Those who know him well will tell you he is well worth knowing, and that is the best biography one can have.

Please Review!

All independent authors depend upon reviews left on Amazon.com by readers to help promote their books. Without these reviews, they will hardly get any notice. Please take the time to leave a short review. Simply go to Amazon.com, find the book and go to the book's page. Under the author's name will be a list of reviews and stars. Click here and there will be a big button saying "Create your own review." Please click here and review.

It only takes a minute!